TEXAS RANGERS

⤜ Legendary Lawmen ⤛

Michael P. Spradlin

Illustrations by Roxie Munro

Walker & Company New York

First published in the United States of America in 2008 by Walker Publishing Company, Inc.
Distributed to the trade by Holtzbrinck Publishers

For information about permission to reproduce selections from this book, write to
Permissions, Walker & Company, 175 Fifth Avenue, New York, New York 10010

Library of Congress Cataloging-in-Publication Data
Spradlin, Michael P.
Texas Rangers : legendary lawmen / Michael P. Spradlin ; illustrations by Roxie Munro.
p.   cm.
ISBN-13: 978-0-8027-8096-6 • ISBN-10: 0-8027-8096-2 (hardcover)
ISBN-13: 978-0-8027-8097-3 • ISBN-10: 0-8027-8097-0 (reinforced)
1. Texas Rangers—History—Juvenile literature. 2. Frontier and pioneer life—Texas—Juvenile literature.
3. Texas Rangers—Biography—Juvenile literature. 4. Texas—History—1846–1950—Juvenile literature.
5. Texas—Biography—Juvenile literature.
I. Munro, Roxie, ill. II. Title.
F391.S77 2008   976.4'063—dc22   2007020139

Typeset in Cushing Book
Art created with India ink and colored inks on Strathmore bristol board
Book design by Michelle Gengaro-Kokmen

Visit Walker & Company's Web site at www.walkeryoungreaders.com

Printed in China
2 4 6 8 10 9 7 5 3 1 (hardcover)
2 4 6 8 10 9 7 5 3 1 (reinforced)

All papers used by Walker & Company are natural, recyclable products
made from wood grown in well-managed forests. The manufacturing processes
conform to the environmental regulations of the country of origin.

This book is for my mom, Vi Spradlin, and her "Group of Jolly Cowboys" with love and affection —M. P. S.

To all my great Texas librarian friends —R. M.

THE BEGINNING

Life on the vast Texas frontier of the 1820s was hard and rugged. Living on small ranches and farms, settlers were often attacked by bandits. And as more people moved onto the Texas plains, the Indian tribes became angry over losing their lands and would often attack settlements. Unable to protect themselves, Texians (as Texans were called before Texas joined the Union in 1845) demanded action from their *alcalde,* or governor, Stephen F. Austin.

Texas was then a part of Mexico, but the government in Mexico City was too far away to offer help. The governor would have to solve this problem alone.

Austin remembered a group of volunteer soldiers who had served in the American Revolutionary War. They were called Minute Men because they were ready to fight at a minute's notice. These

men would leave their homes and shops quickly, gather up their weapons, and march off to battle.

Governor Austin decided Texas needed its own "Minute Men." These volunteers would "range" the frontier to defend Texas whenever danger arose. When the threat had passed, the "ranging companies" would be disbanded, and the volunteers would return to their homes.

In 1823, Governor Austin called the first Ranger Company to duty to defend Texians. Each Ranger provided his own horse and gun. The colonial government supplied ammunition and food for the men and horses whenever possible. Uniforms were not required. Each man dressed for duty as he pleased. This is how the Texas Rangers were born.

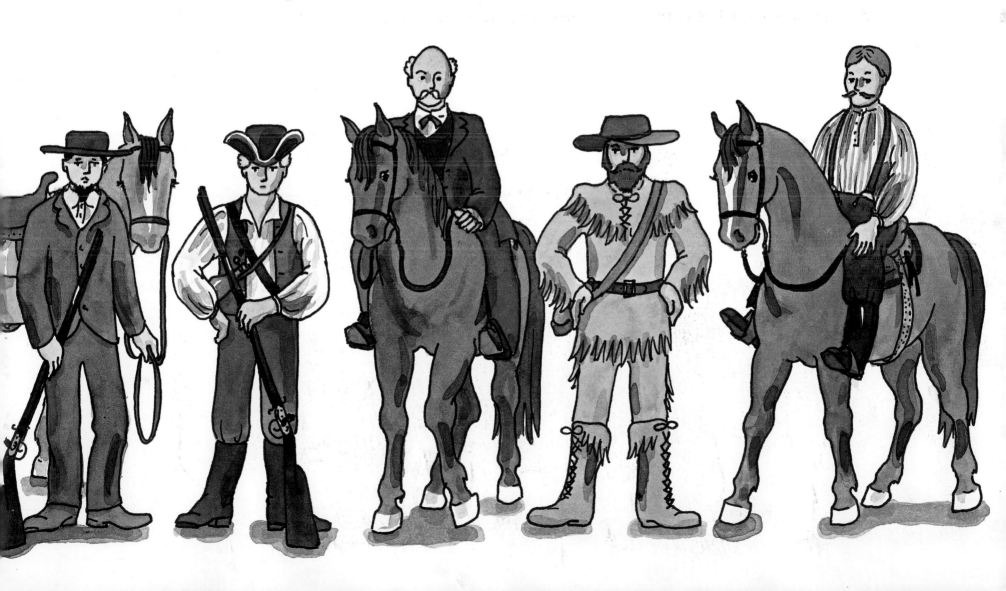

TO THE ALAMO: The Gonzales Ranging Company

In 1836, Texas voted to secede from Mexico and become an independent country. The president of Mexico, General Santa Anna, sent his army north to punish the Texians.

In San Antonio, a small group of soldiers from the Texas Army and a few volunteers from local towns and villages gathered at the Alamo, an old mission near the town. Among the volunteers were the knife fighter Jim Bowie and the equally famous frontiersman Davy Crockett. They waited at the Alamo for the Mexican Army to arrive.

Lieutenant Colonel William Barret Travis, who commanded the Texas Army at the Alamo, sent out several desperate pleas for help. He knew that the small band of soldiers and volunteers would not be powerful enough to hold off the thousands of Mexican soldiers that General Santa Anna was sending their way. Captain John W. Smith of the Texas Army volunteered to ride through the surrounding countryside and ask for help. He left the Alamo and rode to Gonzales, Texas, with news of the coming attack. There, thirty-two men of the Gonzales Ranging Company of Mounted Volunteers answered the call for help.

Captain Smith volunteered to lead the Rangers back to the Alamo. As they neared San Antonio in the early morning, an English-speaking rider appeared out of the darkness. The stranger offered to lead the Rangers through the Mexican lines and into the Alamo.

As they rode on, Captain Smith became suspicious. The Rangers drew their weapons, but before they could shoot, the mysterious rider spurred his horse and rode away. It was a trap! Suddenly, shots rang out!

The Rangers were caught in a desperate cross fire. Thinking they were being attacked in the darkness, the men in the Alamo started shooting at the Rangers, while the Mexican Army fired at them from behind. Dodging bullets, the Rangers finally reached the gates of the Alamo and rode their horses safely inside. Luckily none of the Rangers were injured.

The Gonzales Ranging Company's heroic ride raised the garrison at the Alamo to about 180 men. It was not enough. Before more forces could arrive, the Mexican Army attacked and overthrew the Alamo. All the soldiers and volunteers inside perished in the battle. Only a few civilians survived to tell what had happened there.

THE FIRST FAMOUS RANGER CAPTAIN: John Coffee Hays

John Coffee Hays joined the Rangers in the late 1830s and was appointed to the position of captain in 1840. He was a legend among his men for his courage and leadership.

Shortly after arriving in Texas, Hays purchased a Colt revolving pistol. Each Colt pistol could fire five bullets without reloading. This was a great advantage in gunfights. Whenever he could get them, Captain Hays supplied all of his Rangers with this unique weapon. Forever after, the Colt pistol became a symbol of the Texas Rangers.

In 1841, on patrol near Fredericksburg, Texas, Captain Hays and his Rangers were surprised by a large band of Comanche warriors. In the attack, Hays became separated from his men. Climbing to the top of a nearby hill, he hid himself in a shallow depression.

Alone on the rocky hilltop, he fought off the Comanche for several hours. Each time they charged, Captain Hays's crack shooting drove them back.

Down to his last bullet, Captain Hays was finally rescued by his men. The Comanche came to believe that Captain Hays had magical powers, and this fight became known as "The Battle of Enchanted Rock."

TWO YEARS IN A MEXICAN PRISON: William A. A. "Big Foot" Wallace

William A. A. "Big Foot" Wallace joined the Texas Rangers as a young man. He was nicknamed "Big Foot" because he was a tall man with very large feet.

In 1841, the Mexican Army attacked several settlements in Texas. Wallace and many other Rangers left Texas to chase the army back to Mexico.

After several battles, the Rangers became lost in the desert on their way back to Texas. They ran out of supplies, eating bugs and snakes to stay alive. Desperate for water, they put damp dirt into their mouths, hoping to squeeze out a few drops of moisture. Nearly dead, they were finally captured by the Mexican cavalry and taken to a prison deep in Mexico.

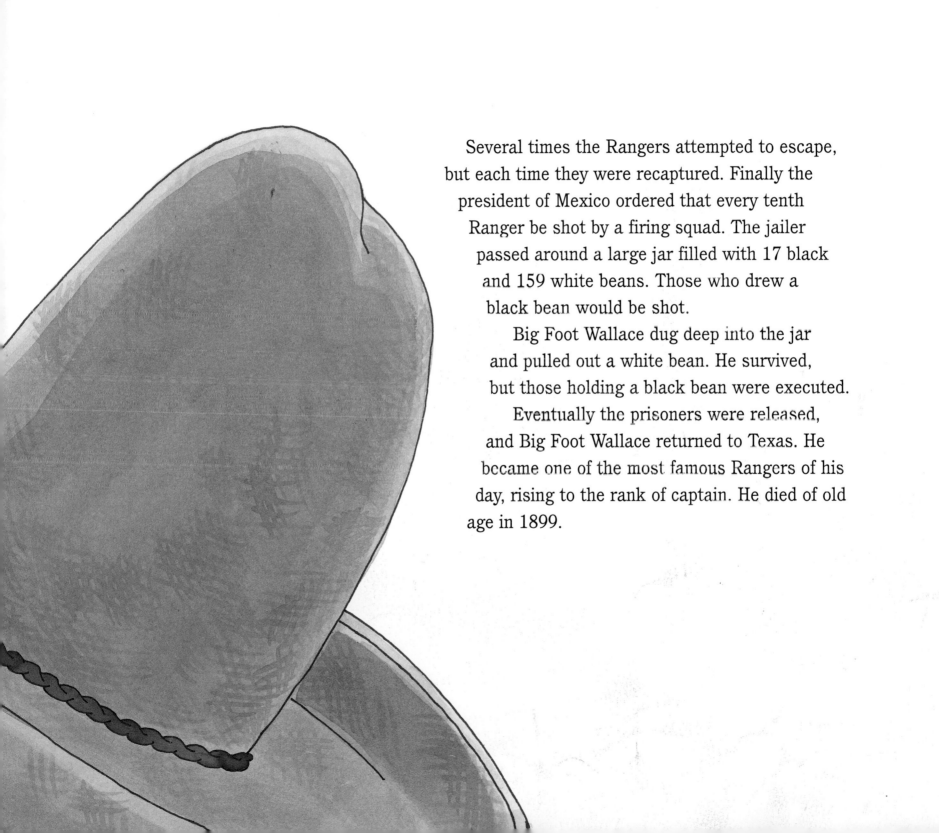

Several times the Rangers attempted to escape, but each time they were recaptured. Finally the president of Mexico ordered that every tenth Ranger be shot by a firing squad. The jailer passed around a large jar filled with 17 black and 159 white beans. Those who drew a black bean would be shot.

Big Foot Wallace dug deep into the jar and pulled out a white bean. He survived, but those holding a black bean were executed.

Eventually the prisoners were released, and Big Foot Wallace returned to Texas. He became one of the most famous Rangers of his day, rising to the rank of captain. He died of old age in 1899.

THE TEXAS DEVILS

In 1845, the Republic of Texas joined the Union. Mexico declared war on the United States. The U.S. Army gathered in Texas to begin the long march toward Mexico City.

Many Texas Rangers joined the army to serve as scouts. Some army officers thought the former Rangers were wild and reckless, but soon they came to respect them as fighters and trackers. During battle, the Texas Rangers often led the attacks.

Rangers would sometimes ride far behind enemy lines, gathering information on the strength of the Mexican troops. Ben McCullough, who had served in Texas as a Ranger captain, was promoted to major in the U.S. Army. On one mission, he led a group of his men deep into enemy territory after nightfall. One by one, he sent them back through the lines with information. Fearing capture at daybreak, Major McCullough disguised himself as a *vaquero*—a Mexican cowboy—by wearing a large sombrero and a serape. Keeping his head down to avoid detection, Major McCullough slowly rode back through the entire Mexican Army, safely reaching the American lines. He was able to give his commanders vital information about the locations and numbers of enemy soldiers.

The former Texas Rangers fought in most of the major battles of the War with Mexico. They were such ferocious fighters that the Mexican soldiers called them *los Diablos Tejanos*— the Texas Devils.

THE FRONTIER BATTALION

When the Civil War ended in 1865, the role of the Texas Rangers began to change from guarding against Indian attacks to protecting Texas citizens from outlaws and bandits. With thousands of new settlers moving into the state, there was an increased need for law and order on the frontier.

In the early 1870s, Ranger companies were sent to patrol the west Texas plains. Ranger captains were allowed to enlist their own troops, usually picking young, unmarried men who owned a good horse. By the middle of the 1880s, even without the danger of Indian attack, it was hazardous work.

Rangers spent many hours on horseback, sometimes covering hundreds of miles in a few days' time. They chased down bank robbers, cattle rustlers, and horse thieves. They were sent into towns to end disputes over local elections and to keep order during important trials.

When not on patrol, Rangers spent time in camp tending to their horses and equipment. Most Rangers carried one or two Colt pistols and a rifle. Target practice, horse racing, and card playing were other popular ways to pass the time in camp.

A few hundred Rangers patrolled thousands of miles of territory. They were tough and determined men. Many times they would leave camp at a moment's notice, riding great distances in pursuit of criminals, never knowing if they would return alive.

For this dangerous duty, most Rangers were paid only $1 a day in wages.

CATCHING OUTLAWS

It is estimated that by age twenty-two, outlaw John Wesley Hardin had killed more than twenty men. Four thousand dollars in reward money was offered for his capture, the largest amount in Texas history. He was a brutal killer with a horrible temper, and he was not afraid to shoot anyone who tried to arrest him.

Local lawmen couldn't capture Hardin, so they asked the Texas Rangers for help. Hardin may not have been afraid of the county sheriff, but he was deathly afraid of the Texas Rangers. He fled Texas immediately.

In 1877, Ranger Sergeant John B. Armstrong was ordered to find and capture Hardin. He tracked Hardin all the way to Pensacola, Florida.

When Hardin heard that Armstrong had arrived in Pensacola, he and a few members of his gang tried to escape by train. Following him to the train station with two local deputies, Armstrong boarded the train and began searching car by car.

Armstrong moved through the train,
studying the eyes of each passenger. Finally
he reached the last car, where the killer sat waiting.

When Sergeant Armstrong entered the car, Hardin
spotted the Colt pistol strapped to the Ranger's hip.
Knowing that the Rangers had arrived, he shouted
out, "Texas by God," as a warning to the other outlaws.
He moved to draw his own pistol, but it became tangled in
his suspenders. Sergeant Armstrong rushed forward, knocking
Hardin unconscious with his Colt.

Sergeant Armstrong dragged Hardin back to Texas in
chains, where Hardin served a long prison term for his crimes.

McNELLY'S RANGERS

In the 1870s, Texas and Mexico's border was a violent, lawless place. Bandits from both sides of the Rio Grande were not afraid to cross the river and rob each other's ranches, banks, and towns. The governor gave Captain Leander McNelly a special commission to raise a company of Rangers and bring law and order to the border. McNelly had served in the Confederate Army during the Civil War and was noted for his bravery and determination.

Captain McNelly enlisted his company of Rangers and made it clear to outlaws on both sides of the river that he was bringing law to the border. When McNelly's Rangers were in pursuit of thieves or rustlers, they did not stop at the Rio Grande but kept going, many times attacking bandit hideouts in Mexico.

When the Mexican government complained about McNelly's border crossing, the government in Washington, D.C., told him to stop invading Mexican territory. Captain McNelly refused, continuing to chase bandits back and forth across the river.

Sickness finally forced Captain McNelly to retire from the Rangers, but not before he had brought some order to the Nueces Strip, along the Rio Grande. For years after, the Rangers who served in McNelly's company called themselves "McNelly's Boys." Leander McNelly is remembered today as one of the bravest Ranger captains in history.

THE LONE WOLF: Manuel T. Gonzaullas

From 1902 to 1920, the state of Texas became the center of the oil industry in America as many major deposits of oil and natural gas were discovered around the state. During these years, the Texas prairie became dotted with oil wells. Wherever oil was discovered, towns began to form, often where no town had been before. These were called boomtowns.

People from all over the country poured into Texas to strike it rich, and criminals and outlaws were not far behind. There was so much crime in some boomtowns that the local lawmen were helpless.

The governor ordered the Texas Rangers to clean up these oil boomtowns. When they entered a town, crime rates plummeted—most often because criminals simply packed up and left.

One of the most famous Rangers of this era was Manuel T. Gonzaullas. Gonzaullas was nicknamed "The Lone Wolf" because he preferred to work alone on his cases. He once said, "I went into lots of fights by myself, and I came out by myself, too!"

Gonzaullas had a unique method of rounding up criminals. When the local jail was full, the Lone Wolf attached a long length of chain to the flagpole in front of the courthouse or jail. Each captured criminal was handcuffed to the chain until he could be brought before a judge. When other crooks saw the men chained to the flagpole, that meant get out of town—fast!

Ranger Gonzaullas eventually rose to the rank of captain. He believed in using scientific methods such as fingerprints to capture outlaws, and he started the first modern laboratory for crime detection in Texas. He went on to solve some of the most famous crimes in Texas history.

BONNIE, CLYDE, AND FRANK

During the Great Depression of the 1930s, Bonnie Parker and Clyde Barrow were two of the most well-known outlaws in the country. Robbing banks all over the South, they became infamous for their narrow escapes and dramatic shoot-outs. In truth, they were vicious criminals who killed and robbed many innocent people.

During this time, the Texas Rangers were caught up in the corruption of Texas politics. Many long-serving Rangers resigned their commissions rather than be part of a corrupt government. One of these men was Captain Frank Hamer.

With Bonnie and Clyde robbing and killing all over Texas, the governor gave Hamer a special commission and asked him to track them down. Captain Hamer and another ex-Ranger, Manny Gault, dedicated their lives to finding Bonnie and Clyde and bringing them to justice.

After months of searching, they tracked the outlaws to a hideout in nearby Louisiana. Taking no chances, the Rangers set up an ambush on a dusty road in the countryside. A rain of Ranger bullets ended the careers of these notorious outlaws. The legend of Bonnie and Clyde lived on, though, as their brief and violent lives were celebrated in songs, books, and movies for decades to follow.

THE TEXAS RANGERS TODAY

The modern Texas Ranger no longer travels on horseback but still serves Texas citizens in preserving life and property. The number of Rangers varies and is established by the Texas state legislature, but in most years about 120 Rangers serve.

The Texas Rangers have included minorities in their ranks almost from the very beginning. Muster rolls from the 1830s show numerous Latino and Native American Rangers serving with companies all over Texas.

While African Americans joined early Ranger companies as teamsters, cooks, and scouts, there is evidence that they also served as Rangers in the early years. In 1988, Sergeant Lee Roy Young Jr. became the first African American member of the modern Texas Rangers.

Women were a part of Ranger history from the early days. In an effort to recruit and maintain the best and most experienced leaders after the Civil War, Ranger captains were allowed to marry. Many captains assigned to the Frontier Battalion took their wives with them to camp while they patrolled the frontier. These Ranger wives were valuable members of the troop. Some were even known to pick up a gun and take part in a shoot-out when things got rough.

In the 1930s, women were given "Special Ranger" appointments and worked in security at the governor's mansion in Austin. In 1993, Sergeant Marrie Garcia was appointed as the first female Ranger of the modern era.

Today, individuals must pass strict oral and written tests to become a Texas Ranger. The Texas Department of Public Safety also requires that applicants live in Texas, have at least eight years of law-enforcement experience in a police agency, and have at least two years of service with the Texas DPS. They must have at least sixty hours of college credit. (Most Rangers have college degrees and some have advanced degrees.) Those who wish to join the Rangers must also be physically fit. Since there are so few Rangers, there are many more applicants than spots available. If you want to be a Ranger and wear the badge and gun with a white or pearl gray Stetson, be prepared for intense competition. When a single spot opens in the ranks, the Texas Department of Public Safety often receives more than one hundred applications to join.

Over nearly two hundred years of history, the men and women who served as Texas Rangers have done so with honor and distinction. Many Rangers have given their lives in defense of their fellow officers and Texas citizens.

In a tradition that began long ago and was given life by Rangers like Captain John Hays, Big Foot Wallace, John B. Armstrong, Leander McNelly, and Lone Wolf Gonzaullas, the duties of the Ranger today are the same. Like their historic counterparts, today's Ranger still wears no official uniform. But while the times and methods may have changed, protecting fellow citizens is still the mission of the Texas Rangers.